FEARSOME, SCARY, AND CREEPY ANIMALS

Fearsome Alligators

Elaine Landau

Enslow Publishers, Inc.

40 Industrial Road   PO Box 38
Box 398   Aldershot
Berkeley Heights, NJ 07922   Hants GU12 6BP
USA   UK

http://www.enslow.com

For Sarah Sutin

Library of Congress Cataloging-in-Publication Data

Landau, Elaine.
  Fearsome alligators / Elaine Landau.
      p. cm. — (Fearsome, scary, and creepy animals)
Summary: Introduces alligators and why they sometimes attack humans, and
tells of some real-life alligator attacks.
  ISBN 0-7660-2060-6 (hardcover : alk. paper)
  1. Alligators—Juvenile literature. 2. Alligator attacks—Juvenile
literature. [1. Alligators. 2. Alligator attacks.] I. Title. II.
Series.
QL666.C925 L35 2003
597.98—dc21   2002006935

Printed in the United States of America

10 9 8 7 6 5 4 3 2 1

To Our Readers:
We have done our best to make sure all Internet addresses in this book were active and appropriate when we went
to press. However, the author and the publisher have no control over and assume no liability for the material
available on those Internet sites or on other Web sites they may link to. Any comments or suggestions can be sent
by e-mail to comments@enslow.com or to the address on the back cover.

Illustration Credits: © 1999 Artville, LLC, pp. 13, 31 (map); © Corel Corporation, pp. ii, iii, 5 (inset), 9, 12, 14
(bottom), 15, 16, 17 (both), 19, 21, 23, 25, 27, 28, 30, 33, 37, 38; Associated Press, p. 8; Bill
Edwards/brandxpictures, pp. 14 (top), 31 (inset); Commander Grady Tuell/National Oceanic & Atmospheric
Administration, p. 24; David Skernick, p. 7; Don Ryan/Associated Press, pp. 11, 34; Getty Images, pp. i, 20–21
(background), 26, 31 (background), 39; Greg Baker/Associated Press, p. 20; Hemera Technologies, Inc., p. 10;
John Bavaro, p. 4; Mark Zimmerman/Associated Press, *The Edmond Sun,* p. 18; Phil Coale/Associated Press,
p. 22; Rudi Von Briel/Index Stock Imagery/PictureQuest, pp. 4–5 (background), 6; Scott Audette/Associated
Press, p. 29; Stephen Morton/Associated Press, p. 35; Wade Spees/Associated Press, p. 36; William
Folsom/National Oceanic & Atmospheric Administration, p. 32. Borders and backgrounds © Corel
Corporation, unless otherwise noted.

Cover Illustration: Getty Images

Contents

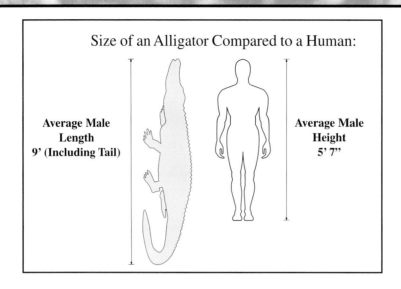

Size of an Alligator Compared to a Human:

Average Male Length 9' (Including Tail)

Average Male Height 5' 7"

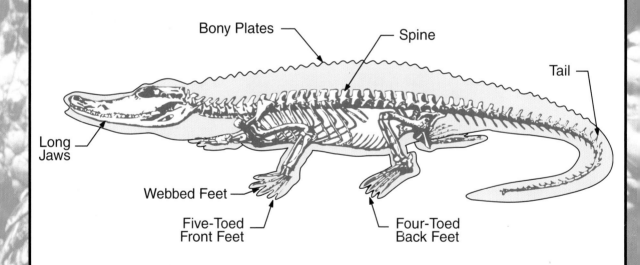

Bony Plates

Spine

Tail

Long Jaws

Webbed Feet

Five-Toed Front Feet

Four-Toed Back Feet

Alligators look like lizards, but they are much larger, with thicker bodies and tails.

1. A Family Outing

It started out as a beautiful July day. The Teixeira family had gone to Shark Valley, part of Everglades National Park, in Florida. The weather was perfect for biking. The family rode on a trail along the water. It seemed as if nothing would spoil the day.

No one could have expected what would happen next. Seven-year-old Alexandre lost control of his bike. He fell into the murky water.

Alexandre never had a chance to get out. An alligator appeared almost instantly. It swam toward Alexandre. The alligator opened its huge mouth.

Florida's Everglades National Park is a swampy area that is filled with animals such as alligators, deer, fish, snakes, pelicans, and even Florida panthers.

The long front part of the alligator's head is called the snout. The alligator's eyes stick up from the snout so that it can see while the rest of its body is underwater.

It clamped its jaws around the little boy's body.

The boy's father leaped into the water. He wanted to save his son. Alexandre's father grabbed the alligator's snout. That is the long front part of an alligator's head. He tried to open its jaws. But that was impossible. So he just clung to the animal. He had to keep the alligator where it was. Alexandre's father knew what would happen if it swam away. Alexandre would drown, and then he would be eaten.

It was terrifying. At one point, the father felt the alligator slipping away. It was dragging Alexandre under the water. To his relief, the alligator came right back up. The standoff continued. The alligator would not let go of Alexandre. And Alexandre's father would not let go of the alligator.

Alexandre's mother came running into the water. She tried to help her husband. She pushed her hand into the alligator's mouth. She hoped this would make it let go of her child. The animal did open its mouth, but it bit the

Alligators have powerful jaws and many sharp teeth. Once an alligator clamps its jaws down on its prey, it can be difficult for the victim to escape.

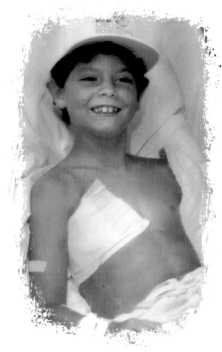

Alexandre Teixeira survived the alligator attack thanks to his parents' quick thinking and the treatment he received at Miami Children's Hospital.

woman's hand. It tried to draw her in, too. Then suddenly it let them both go.

The horror was over. Alexandre was taken to Miami Children's Hospital. Surprisingly, his injuries were not serious. The doctors promised a speedy recovery.

Alexandre is a lucky boy. Everglades National Park is alligator country. Many people go there hoping to see an alligator. But no one wants to swim with one. The alligator that attacked Alexandre was not hunting for children. But Alexandre's fall probably startled it. It may have thought the boy was its prey, or food. So it attacked.

Most alligators do not attack humans.

Alligators in the Everglades do not usually attack humans, but sometimes they may mistake people for their prey. This is why it is important to know how dangerous these animals can be, and treat them with the proper respect.

Yet accidents do happen. More accidents have occurred lately. There may be a good reason for this. The number of alligators is on the rise.

When our nation was young, there were many alligators. But over the years, their numbers lessened due to hunting. Alligators were hunted for their skins.

People hunted alligators to use their skins to make briefcases, shoes, bags, and other items.

People used these to make boots, belts, and purses. By the 1950s, alligators were almost completely wiped out.

The government tried to help. In time, alligators were protected by law. It is now illegal to harm these animals. A special permit is needed to hunt or trap them. These steps helped. Today, there is no shortage of alligators.

But in many places, there is no shortage of people, either. New communities have sprung up. Others have grown larger. Sometimes these communities are near where alligators live. This raises an important question. Can alligators and people live near each other?

It is possible. But first, the humans have to learn

It is natural to want to see where alligators live, but you should always stay at a safe distance. These children are standing far enough from the alligator to prevent an attack.

a few rules. They cannot feed wild alligators. This changes the animal's natural behavior. Alligators should never connect people with food. That can make them very dangerous. In some areas, feeding a wild alligator is against the law.

No one should ever try to touch a wild alligator, either. This is true even if the animal is asleep. Never get closer to an alligator than fifteen feet. If it hisses, you should back off even further. An alligator will never be a loving pet.

It is also best to stay out of waters where there are alligators. Wading, swimming, or water-skiing there is risky. Small children should not play on these shores.

Alligators are wild animals. They are naturally

Alligators can be found in lakes, swamps, and rivers along the Gulf of Mexico.

fearful of humans. It is important that they stay this way. Accidents will probably still happen. But hopefully, they will happen less often.

2. All About Alligators

Alligators are amazing animals. They have been on Earth for more than 65 million years. Alligators were here when dinosaurs roamed the land. They remain almost unchanged since then.

Today there are two types of alligators: American alligators and Chinese alligators. American

Chinese alligators (above) are smaller than American alligators (below).

alligators are large. The males are usually between eleven and twelve feet long. They can weigh almost 1,000 pounds. The largest females are about nine feet long. They weigh over 150 pounds. Chinese alligators are smaller. They only grow to about six feet. There are fewer than 200 Chinese alligators left in the world.

All alligators are reptiles. Reptiles are cold-blooded animals. They are not spiteful or cruel. Being cold-blooded has to do with body temperature. A cold-blooded animal's body temperature changes with its surroundings. In colder weather, an alligator's body temperature drops. When it is very warm, its body temperature rises.

Some people compare alligators to lizards. They say that alligators look like monster lizards. That is because alligators are so much

Lizards, like this one, are much smaller than alligators.

Alligators are strong swimmers and can move quickly in the water.

bigger than lizards. Alligators also have broader bodies than lizards. Their tails are broader, too.

An alligator's tail is important in the water. These animals swim by moving their tails from side to side. They also have four short but strong legs. An alligator's feet are helpful both on land and in the water. The animal's back feet are webbed and have four toes. These help it steer in the water. Its front feet have five long toes. These give the alligator firm footing on the ground.

Many people think alligators are bright green. But only the alligators in Hollywood movies are that color.

Adult alligators are usually gray, deep olive, or black in color.

Young alligators are actually dark brown or black. They have yellow bands or marks on their bodies.

As the alligator ages, the marks fade. Adult alligators are usually dull gray, deep olive (a yellowish green), or black. They are often mistaken for logs floating in the water.

An alligator's skin is tough. There are bony plates

Alligators floating in the water sometimes look like logs.

within the skin. That makes the alligator's body look "armored." But the scariest part of an alligator is probably its mouth. These reptiles have eighty-two sharp, cone-shaped teeth. Beneath each tooth is a replacement tooth. Damaged or worn teeth fall out. New ones replace them.

Alligators have very sharp teeth.

Alligators can swim with only their eyes showing above the surface of the water.

The alligator's eyes are on top of its skull. This can be quite useful. The alligator can see above the water. It does this while the rest of its body is underwater. So alligators can see you before you see them. Look out!

3. Feeding Time

It is after dark. But the animal night-hunters are awake. They are looking for food. Alligators are among them. These reptiles begin to hunt after the sun goes down.

Alligators are fierce predators. A predator is an animal that kills and eats other animals for food. Most other animals usually do not prey on adult alligators. However, large alligators sometimes eat smaller ones. Otherwise, humans are their only enemies.

Alligators are fierce predators.

Tonight, there is a hungry alligator in a large Louisiana lake. It is looking for a meal. Soon, it finds what it wants. The alligator spots a small deer at the water's edge. The deer has stopped there for a drink.

The alligator silently swims toward it. The deer does not see it coming until it is too late. The alligator grips the deer's leg with its mouth. Its strong jaws and sharp teeth tightly hold the victim. The deer struggles. But it is no use—it cannot escape. The alligator quickly drags the deer beneath the water. The deer drowns.

Now the alligator is ready to eat the deer. But alligators do not chew their food. Their teeth are made

Alligators sometimes attack much larger animals, such as deer.

for grasping and holding, not chewing. They swallow their prey whole.

But a deer is too big to eat that way. So the alligator spins and twists the deer's body. It slams the dead animal against the shore. The alligator uses its sharp teeth and strong jaw muscles to break the deer's bones. Finally, it rips off a piece of the deer. The piece is small enough to swallow. At last, the alligator can eat its kill.

An alligator cannot always rip its prey apart. When this happens, the alligator waits for the

Alligators do not chew their food—they swallow it whole.

meat to rot. This usually takes a few days. At that point, it is soft enough to tear.

Alligators do not just eat wild animals. Sometimes, they prey on pets. This is especially true of dogs.

It happened to one dog in Seminole, Florida. The dog was a Dalmatian puppy named Sandi. Sandi belonged to the Callaway family. There were three young girls in the family, as well.

The Callaways lived near Lake Seminole. One evening, Sandi ran down to the lake. The puppy liked to play in the water. She chased the ducks there.

The three sisters followed the dog. They watched her from the wooden dock. Then the

Sandi, a Dalmatian puppy like this one, was attacked by an alligator in Seminole, Florida.

Alligators can move quickly on land, as well as in the water.

girls spotted an alligator. It was a large one, and it was swimming toward Sandi.

The children called out to their dog. The oldest girl, Cassandra, tossed sticks in the water to get Sandi's attention. But the puppy did not notice.

The alligator picked up speed. Seconds later, it had

Sandi in its jaws. It pulled the dog under. "I don't think she saw it coming," Cassandra said.

It all happened quickly. The Callaway children lost their dog. They were heartbroken. And what happened to Sandi is not uncommon.

But not all the dogs attacked by alligators die. Some live through it. A few even become heroes. Blue, another dog from Florida, is among these.

One night, eighty-five-year-old Ruth

Gay took Blue for a walk. It had been raining, and the grass was still wet. Mrs. Gay slipped and fell. She broke her nose and hurt her shoulder. Ruth Gay could not get up. She lay on the ground waiting for help to come. Blue stayed by her side.

Suddenly, the elderly woman heard Blue growling. It was very dark. She could not see what was happening. She could only hear the dog yelping and whining. She thought Blue was in a fight.

Mrs. Gay was right. Blue was fighting off an

Alligators are not easy creatures to fight, but Blue managed to protect his owner.

alligator. It had crept out of a nearby canal. The dog was determined to protect the injured woman. He would not leave her.

The alligator badly wounded Blue. But somehow the small dog escaped its grasp. Finally, the large reptile left. It never touched Mrs. Gay.

Blue was patched up by a veterinarian, a doctor who takes care of animals. He was very proud of Blue. The veterinarian said, "It's amazing what an animal will do in a time of need. He's a pretty brave dog."

4. A Scary Night Out

No one expects an alligator attack. People are always surprised when it happens. But it happens more often than people think.

It happened to a fourteen-year-old girl named Edna Wilks. Edna was from Orlando, Florida. One night, she and five friends went swimming. They were having a great time at a local lake. Some of the teens were relaxing on body boards. These are lightweight boards that you can float on in the water.

Alligators can move silently through the water and strike before you know they are there.

Suddenly, Edna felt something tug

at her arm. She fell off her body board and into the water. At first, she thought that it was her friends. They were always fooling around. But it was not her friends—it was an alligator.

Edna was terrified. She started to scream. The large reptile spun her around in the water. Then she heard a loud crack. It was her arm. It had snapped in the alligator's mouth.

"He was spinning me around in the water real fast and jerking me," Edna said. "I was thinking—this is how I am going to die. I'm going to drown in a minute."

Finally, the spinning stopped. The alligator came to the surface. Edna

With help from her friend, Amanda Valance, Edna escaped from the alligator.

was able to breathe. However, her arm was still in the alligator's mouth. She fought to save herself. The teenage girl used her free hand to pull on the reptile's jaw. Finally, the alligator let go.

One of Edna's friends helped her get back on the body board. Then, Edna's friend pulled the board to shore. The alligator trailed behind them. They were glad that was where it stayed.

Luckily, Edna soon recovered. She is very grateful to her friend for helping her get away from the alligator.

5. An Alligator's Life

People everywhere tell alligator stories. But these reptiles do not live everywhere. In the United States, American alligators are found from North Carolina to Florida. They also live along the Gulf Coast. The Chinese alligator lives in China's Yangtze River Valley.

Alligators are largely freshwater animals. They can be found in swamps, marshes, rivers, and lakes. Alligators may also be spotted in canals and ponds. They sometimes

Chinese alligators live along the Yangtze River.

Swampy areas like this one in Florida are often homes for alligators.

live in brackish (salty) water, as well.

In cold weather, alligators go into a rest period. This may last a few months. Some stay in hollows or tunnels they dig in the mud. These are called "gator holes." A gator hole may be as long as sixty-five feet. It protects the alligator from the cold. Alligators also use gator holes during droughts. These are important when the water level drops. The hollows still have water. So the alligators remain comfortable.

Alligators are mostly carnivorous. That means they are meat eaters. Alligators eat both land and water animals. These include fish, snakes, frogs, and turtles. Alligators also eat birds and raccoons.

Large male alligators often eat even bigger animals. They attack dogs, cows, pigs, and deer. Baby alligators feed on insects, snails, and small fish. However, alligators are not picky eaters. They have even been known to eat aluminum cans, fishing lures, stones, and sticks.

Alligators eat many types of small animals, such as frogs.

Reproduction

Alligators reproduce or multiply when they mature. This takes place when they are about ten to twelve years old. By then, they are usually about six feet long.

The alligator-breeding season is from April to May. After mating, the females build nests. They usually pick a marshy area for this. The nests are shaped like a mound. They are made of sticks, grass, pieces of plants, and mud. Alligator nests are large. They measure about seven feet across. They may be as high as three-and-a-half feet. Females lay their eggs in late June and early July.

Alligators usually mate in a marshy area.

They lay from twenty to sixty eggs in the center of the nest.

Alligator nests, like this one, are built by the female.

Female alligators are not like birds. They do not sit on their nests. They would crack the eggs. Instead, the female alligator covers her eggs with a top layer of mud and grasses. The female then remains close to the nest. She protects it from predators. Raccoons often raid alligator nests to eat the eggs.

After nine or ten weeks, the eggs hatch. The baby alligators make high-pitched sounds. This alerts the mother. She digs them out of the nest. Then, the female usually carries them to the water.

Young alligators are called hatchlings. At birth, they measure between eight and ten inches long. The young alligators often remain together in a group. This is known as a pod. The alligators in a pod stay close to the adult female. Sometimes, they sit on her head and back. Hatchlings may remain with their mother for as long as two years.

Although baby alligators may look cute, you should never attempt to touch one—its mother could be close by. The person holding this alligator is a trained expert.

She will try to protect them from other animals who might kill and eat them.

But many hatchlings still die. Raccoons, snakes, otters, large fish, wading birds, and other animals prey on baby alligators. Only one out of every ten alligators lives through its first year.

Those are not good odds. But alligators have

Only one out of every ten alligators lives to become an adult.

nevertheless survived. If unharmed by humans, they will continue to do so.

It is important to leave alligators in the wild alone. They can be seen and enjoyed elsewhere. Many zoos have alligators. In some parts of the country, there are alligator farms. Often these places give tours. There are

You can see alligators in their natural habitats on a tour through the Everglades.

also guided tours through Florida's Everglades. On a warm day, you can see many alligators. Books and films about alligators can also be found there.

Alligators are fascinating. They are among the most powerful reptiles alive. We can study and admire them. Yet it is always best to do so from a distance. We do not need to fear alligators, but we must respect them.

Fast Facts About ALLIGATORS

❖ The alligator is the second largest reptile in the United States. Only the American crocodile is bigger.

❖ American Indians once wore alligator teeth around their necks. They thought that the alligator teeth would ward off bad luck.

❖ Alligators in zoos may live from sixty to eighty years. In the wild, alligators usually only live from thirty-five to fifty years.

❖ The longest alligator on record was nineteen feet, two inches long. It came from Louisiana. This alligator was trapped in the early 1900s.

❖ Alligators look slow, but they can be fast on their feet. They can reach speeds of up to twenty miles per hour for short distances.

❖ Alligator teeth are often shed and replaced. Old alligators may have had as many as fifty sets of teeth.

❖ Early Spanish explorers called the alligator *el lagarto*. It means "the lizard."

❖ The alligator has been named Florida's state reptile.

❖ A healthy alligator can go for months without eating. These reptiles store fat in their bodies and tails.

❖ An alligator can survive in water as cold as 36 degrees Fahrenheit or as warm as 98 degrees Fahrenheit.

Glossary

brackish   Salty.

carnivorous   Meat-eating.

cold-blooded An animal whose body temperature changes with its surroundings.

fade   To lighten in color.

hatchlings   Alligator young.

illegal   Against the law.

mature   To age or become older.

permit   A document that gives permission to do something.

pod   A group of alligator young.

predator   An animal that hunts other animals for food.

prey	An animal that is hunted by another animal as food.
reproduce	To multiply or create young.
reptile	A cold-blooded animal (see above). Reptiles either walk on four short legs or crawl along the ground.
snout	The long front part of an alligator's head.
ton	A unit of weight equaling 2,000 pounds.
veterinarian	A doctor who takes care of animals.
wading	Walking through water.

Further Reading

Dudley, Karen. *Alligators and Crocodiles*. Austin, TX: Raintree Steck-Vaughn, 1998.

Fitzgerald, Patrick J. *Croc and Gator Attacks*. Danbury, CT: Children's Press, 2000.

Lauber, Patricia. *Alligators: A Success Story*. New York: Henry Holt, 1993.

Ling, Mary. *Amazing Crocodiles and Reptiles*. (Eyewitness Juniors) New York: DK Publishing, 1991.

Markle, Sandra. *Outside and Inside Alligators*. New York: Atheneum, 1998.

Ricciuti, Edwards R. *Reptiles*. Woodbridge, CT: Blackbirch Press, 1993.

Richardson, Joy. *Reptiles*. Danbury, CT: Franklin Watts, 1993.

Simon, Seymour. *Crocodiles and Alligators*. New York: Harper Collins, 1999.

Staub, Frank J. *Alligators*. Minneapolis, MN: Lerner Publications, 1995.

Woodward, John. *Crocodiles and Alligators*. Tarrytown, NY: Marshall Cavendish, 1999.

Internet Sites

St. Augustine's Alligator Park—Zoological Park

Take an online tour of this fun alligator farm. Enjoy great pictures and learn why alligators are special. There is a lot to see here.

<http://www.alligatorfarm.com>

All About Alligators—Enchanted Learning Software

Learn interesting facts about alligators and their relatives.

<http://enchantedlearning.com/subjects/reptiles/

alligator/Alligator.shtml>

Index